Confrontation Skills

How to Argue and Win Every Time

by

Rhonda Scharf

©2014 by Rhonda Scharf
ISBN 9781515218975 Published by MHW Communications

Contents

Chapter One: What Is Confrontation?

I define confrontation as tension in a relationship. A situation will build until it reaches a point where somebody feels they need to say something. So confrontation is the need to have a conversation.

There are different degrees of confrontation. There is a nice friendly conversation, like, "It bugs me when you do this." Then there are higher degrees of confrontation, usually when people wait too long to have the conversation, and by the time they need to have a confrontation, it's escalated — at least in one person's mind — to something that's quite a bit larger than it might have been otherwise.

The quick and simple definition of confrontation is "tension that needs to be addressed." Most people don't enjoy it at all. It's an uncomfortable conversation. It doesn't matter how many times you have to have a confrontation, it's never fun.

Obviously there are right ways to do it, and in this book I'm going to be talking about those right ways and walking you through what you need to do, how you need to do it, when you need to do it.

You're never really going to like doing it or even get comfortable doing it. But it's a conversation that needs to happen so that the relationship can move forward. By ignoring a confrontation you are allowing the situation to escalate and it will damage the relationship. Confrontation (done properly) is damage control or relationship management.

Although I use a lot of workplace examples, I will use some general life examples as well. You can, for example, have confrontation in your family. You might need to say to a family member, "It really bugs me when you don't show up at my house on time." That could be a conversation, but it could feel very filled with tension, more like con*front*ation.

As humans, we all have four basic psychological needs. Tension is created when one of those psychological needs have been violated. That tension is conflict.

The need to be valued

The first psychological need is the need to be valued. If someone feels unappreciated, taken for granted, or just through a plain lack of recognition, it will create the fear or anger response, and that fear or anger response is the tension.

Let's say you are working for someone and they never say thank you, or they never say that you're doing a good job. Over time you start to feel that you are not appreciated for what you do and it causes you to say to yourself, "What am I — chopped liver?" The lack of recognition says that your need to be valued isn't being met by the other person and creates a tension that one person is aware of, but possibly the other person is not.

In our home life it happens all the time as well (again, usually innocently, or one-sided). Mom goes to work all day, and when she comes home she rushes to get dinner on the table.

Every once in a while things don't go according to plan; something gets burned, or doesn't taste right and one of the kids will complain about it. That will immediately make Mom feel like no one in the family values all the effort it takes to make meals daily. There will likely be a tension at the table and potentially Mom may get angry, or even cry. She perceives the criticism of the dinner as not being appreciated (or valued) by the family.

Tension.

Typically, the other person (in this case, the kids) has no idea why Mom is upset. The tension is one-sided, but it affects the relationship.

The need for self-esteem

The second psychological need is the need for self-esteem. We need to feel good about ourselves. When people poke fun, or they make us the butt of the joke or of their sarcasm, it feels as if our self-esteem is being taken away. It's almost as if we're chopped off at the knees. So, naturally, that creates tension. Now, in every really good relationship, best friends might well greet each other with insult banter. But work colleagues typically don't. When someone says something to you at work such as, "Oh, nice of you to join us. Did we get in the way of your nap time?" It feels as if they're trying to take away your credibility or, to a certain degree, your self-esteem. Professionally — how you do your job — if not emotionally. When that has been compromised, it causes conflict.

When the relationship is very healthy, this banter is seen as fun. When the relationship already has some tension, it feels much more like an attack.

We need to have a conversation when these things happen so we can keep the relationship healthy. No confrontation = unhealthy relationship and even the little things (such as "She walked right by me and didn't even say hello!") become much larger in scale and damage.

NO CONFRONTATION = TENSION = UNHEALTHY RELATIONSHIP

9

The Need to be Fair

The third psychological need is the need to be fair. I find it fascinating that although we are all adults, we all have an overwhelming need for the world to be fair. Even though we know that that makes no sense, when something isn't perceived as fair, it will create tension.

Assume there is a new job posting at work that you are qualified for. A co-worker wins the competition, even though you've been there ten years longer than they have. You probably will feel that isn't fair as you have been there longer. Tension will be present in that relationship, even if just for a short time. Again, that's often a one-way tension because the other person may not be aware of it.

In my family we have regular family gatherings for birthdays, Thanksgiving, Christmas etc., and every once in a while it really bothers me that they are always at our house. I get frustrated that all the work ends up in my lap. It really isn't fair that it is always me putting on these large dinners and I will get frustrated with my brother or other family members for never offering to host them.

That actually combines with the need to be valued, because sometimes I get annoyed that no one ever really acknowledges all the work (or expense) required for such large family gatherings.

I don't think it is fair, and I don't feel appreciated for all that I do.

If I say something about it, then I am dealing with the tension and hopefully I will either feel appreciated for all I do, or someone else will offer to host the event, making it feel a little fairer to me.

If I don't say anything, I'm letting the tension build, and I am in danger of exploding at the wrong time accusing everyone of taking advantage of me (and potentially sounding like a four-year-old having a temper tantrum with a statement such as "It's not fair that it is always me!") The odds are that my family members would never see the explosion coming and feel threatened, certainly causing even more tension.

Since I am the one who feels the tension (because my need to be fair has been violated from my perspective), I must say something. It doesn't have to be in a confrontational manner at all, but I do have to say something.

Now when a family gathering comes up, I say to my brother, "Since I had Christmas and Easter at our house, I think that you should host the Mother's Day event. Does that sound fair to you?"

The Need to be in Control

The fourth and final psychological need is the need to be in control. This one is actually the most common, as we are all control freaks about some things, just to different degrees.

Perhaps you consider yourself "set in your ways" about things. That is a control issue. Maybe you're a little more black and white than others. That is seen as control by others as well.

It could be something quite simple, such as the way we create documents, or the font, or the language that we use. It might be about the way you load the dishwasher, cut the grass or wash the car. Everyone is a control freak about something.

However, you may not realize how much tension this actually causes.

When I was much younger, I worked for a micro-manager boss. He had high control needs, and I have fairly high control needs as well. They naturally clashed.

He was a big believer in time logs, reports, measurements and communication. I perceived each of those reports as my having to report that I worked each day, and that I wasn't wasting time. I resented filling them in. Tension.

On the days he was out of the office, he would call five minutes before quitting time to check in.

In hindsight I realize that he was just ensuring the day went smoothly, and that there were no emergencies to be dealt with (long before the day of the cell phone). He wanted to control that the office ran smoothly (which was really one of his functions as manager).

I perceived (at the time) that he was calling to check up on me, to ensure that I was still in the office and hadn't skipped out early. I felt

13

his micro-managing ways showed that he didn't trust me at all. Tension.

From my perspective, I felt that his need to control me took away my need to control me. I felt like I was being treated like a child. It not only violated my need for personal control, it also violated my need to feel valued (and appreciated), my self-esteem (because I felt like

I was being treated as not trustworthy), and the need for fairness (because he didn't call everyone else – just me).

Now that I'm older I look back at some of the things that I did at the time to exercise my own control and wince. A nice simple conversation about the issue would have clarified that it wasn't a trust issue at all. So much tension and resentment could have been alleviated if I had just sat down and chatted with him about how I was feeling.

When any one of those psychological needs is violated, it creates tension and tension creates conflict. You need to have a conversation or a confrontation to alleviate the tension.

It is important that we look at both sides of the situation, and see what the other person is experiencing as well. Perhaps we are violating the other person's needs by our actions. It helps defuse some tension in advance.

When my older son Christopher was going through those difficult teenage years, we had more than one confrontation. If I took the time to look at the situation from his perspective, it was so much easier for me to deal with.

Mom:	Chris, it is eight o'clock at night. Where are you going? Don't you have homework?
Chris:	Out.
Mom:	Out where?
Chris:	Side.

If I look at that conversation from Christopher's point of view, he feels as if I am taking away his control, and potentially his need for self-esteem. He is old enough to know that he needs to do his homework, and resents that I am even questioning him on something is capable of taking care of on his own. He feels as if I am trying to control him by needing to know where he is at every moment of the day. He is exercising his need for control by taking away some of mine.

I'm not saying that as a parent I don't have the right to ask those questions. I am saying that if I can see where the tension is coming from, I can perhaps reduce it by how I deal with the situation.

Mom:	Chris, it's eight o'clock at night and you're going out? At night I need to know where you are going so I don't worry about you (explaining myself helps remove the appearance of control).
Chris:	Out.
Mom:	I'll assume your homework is done, and I would appreciate you being home by 10:00. (Not insisting, although as a parent I have that right. This will reduce some of the tension of imposing a curfew).

That still may not be perfect, but I can still exercise my need for control without completely removing his. I never intended to indicate to him that I didn't think he could do his homework, so I'll take the high road and not push the homework issue.

Being aware that needs are easily violated on both sides of a tension-filled situation allows us to be a bit more proactive in avoiding causing these situations.

Examine which of your needs have been

Violated, as this helps you realize where the tension is coming from, and how to start the conversation about dealing with it.

Having an honest look to see if your actions have violated the needs of the other person will enable you to approach the situation clearly.

In my previous book *Dealing with Difficult People* I explain how situations are never one sided. There are always two sides to the story; two people involved. In order to deal with a confrontation effectively, you must look at the situation from the other perspective as well.

Chapter Two: Three Stages of Conflict

In order to create our strategy for dealing with our confrontation, we must arm ourselves with as much information about the situation as we can. By determining the severity of the conflict (or tension), we can decide if we want a conversation or if a direct confrontation is required.

I have narrowed it down to basically three stages of conflict. Logic would tell you that all conflict starts at the first level and escalates to the second and then the third, but that isn't necessarily true. The levels are not always sequential, and conflict doesn't always start at the first level.

Sometimes situations are so intense that they result in a needed confrontation immediately (think a situation on the highway where you've been cut off, or someone is driving dangerously). A nice conversation isn't going to alleviate the tension in that situation.

Sometimes the situations are minor and never escalate beyond that (think when someone at work leaves their lunch containers in the fridge for months at a time). A big confrontation is probably overkill for that situation.

By identifying the stage of conflict, and the potential to escalate, you can decide whether a confrontation or a conversation is required.

Stage One

The first stage of conflict is the accumulation of little annoyances; those everyday things that get in the way. The no-big-deal stuff. The day-to-day irritations. It is where we are uncomfortable and potentially even annoyed, but we're quick to dismiss or justify these behaviors.

It might be someone at work walking away from the photocopier when it's jammed, or always taking the last cup of coffee. At home, it might be not replacing the toilet paper roll.

It's the small stuff that makes you wonder whether you should even talk to the other person about it. You feel as if you're making a really big deal out of something that isn't that important. Most people tend to dismiss that, but sometimes it builds.

Some of those stage one level of conflict situations never go any further. The next day, the fact that they left the coffee empty doesn't bother you. You think, "Oh, they're just lazy," and it doesn't bug you today, even though yesterday you were ready to bite their head off for the same thing! So in those cases, sometimes it doesn't go anywhere.

Now, I believe the first stage of conflict is really where the conversation happens, and if we were much more comfortable having a conversation at this stage, we could potentially avoid a lot of confrontations.

Certainly, you don't need to have a conversation about every single thing, or you'll be perceived as a very difficult person. (You'll need my other book to make sure you aren't!) When the situation gets to that point when you realize this has bothered you three times in a row, or it's clearly something that's not going to stop, then you may feel you have to say something. Then you have the conversation. If you don't, often the tension will continue to build, with potential consequences.

Sometimes things don't start as the little annoyances of the first level but go right into the second level.

Stage Two

The second level is more significant. Whatever is happening is not a minor irritation like the coffee pot being left empty. Stage two conflict takes on a level of competition, and it feels as if one person is going to win and one person is going to lose.

It starts to feel very personal when we are in stage two. That's why, when we get to the second level of conflict, we're no longer dealing with a conversation, but an actual confrontation. And because it feels very personal, it's much more nerve-wracking and emotional.

This is where we start to play the cover-your butt game.

In the first stage, you're not likely to send someone an email saying, "Look, you left the coffee empty again." You're more likely to see them in the hall and say, "I notice you left the coffee pot empty again. Do you think your mom works here?" Sometimes our approach is a little sarcastic, and potentially unprofessional. We try to cover our confrontation in humour thinking it makes the situation easier to deal with. In stage one, we are annoyed by the behaviour, but don't tend to feel that it is a personal attack.

However, once we hit the second level, we often will move to email confrontation, because we want a paper trail so that if it does blow up, we can show evidence saying, "Look, I was really nice here."

In fact, email is probably one of the worst things you can do once a situation has turned personal. We read emails based on relationship and if there is a negative tension in the relationship, we will read the email with a negative tone. When we write the email we may not have input the negative tone, but that is exactly how it will be read by the other person.

Stage two of conflict becomes a battle. Me vs You. Us vs Them. It becomes very people-focused. It's not hostile. It's not in the danger zone yet, but it can become very sarcastic. People try to laugh the sarcasm off as jokes, but it still feels personal and tense.

Assume you are expected to be in a meeting at 2:00pm, but you were tied up on a conference call until 2:15pm.

Mike might be in that meeting, and you and Mike are not the best of friends. For whatever reason, there is tension in your relationship that has not been addressed. When you enter the meeting, Mike might say "Oh, nice of you to join us. Did we get in the way of your nap time?" or something similar. There's a lot of sarcasm and public jabbing disguised as humour in stage two.

It is quite understandable that you take this personally. You feel that Mike (and everyone else) is laughing at you; embarrassing you for being late, and taking away your right to even explain why you were late. Tension between you and Mike has just risen a notch higher.

When you relate this to the four psychological needs that I spoke about in Chapter One, the need to be fair and the need to be in control have just been violated by Mike.

He is making you the butt of his joke, which isn't fair because you were on a conference call, and he is taking away your control to even explain why you are late. Potentially, he is violating your self-esteem as it feels that everyone is laughing at you.

Each of these is a very personal need, which is why the second level of conflict feels so personal. It feels like Mike is attacking you. As I said, the second stage of conflict is not hostile, and it's not dangerous for a relationship, but there's potential danger depending on how you handle it. It's at this level we really do need to say something. Ignoring this would say to Mike that is okay for him to do that again in the future; when in fact, it is not okay.

Hopefully, you can have it in a conversation. Hopefully, it's nice and conversational. "I don't know if you're aware of this, but if I walk into a meeting late because I've been on a conference call and you point out that I'm late, I find that really embarrassing, and I'd appreciate if you didn't do that."

Mike might say, "Relax. I was just making a joke." It could be a conversation that feels a little confrontational, because you're asking them to stop doing something.

Or it could be much more of a "we need to sit down and talk about this, because it's going to escalate if we don't" type of situation.

The danger with the second level of conflict is that if you ignore the situation, it will escalate. At the first level it doesn't necessarily escalate, but at the second level it will, because it gets under your skin and eats away at you causing you to retaliate in some way.

BEHAVIOUR NOT ADDRESSED IS
PERMISSION TO CONTINUE

Let's look at some things you can do to prevent escalation at the second level.

First of all, when you have a person who pushes your buttons — whether it's fairness or control or self-esteem or value — you need to be very strategic.

When you're entering a situation where that person is going to be, you need to say to yourself things like, "Okay, don't get baited. Don't jump back. Don't attack back." This helps you make sure that you're in control of your reactions. If you forget to remind yourself, you might do or say something you regret. By reminding yourself, you are more likely to have more control.

Here's a good tip. If you're sitting at a boardroom table, you should always sit beside the person you don't like.

The natural instinct is to sit far away from them, and then watch them. Then when you say something, you might see them whispering to the person beside them and you will think, "They're talking about me."

But if they're sitting right beside you, you won't even think they're talking about you because you are right there. You don't have to chat. You don't have to pretend. But your paranoia level goes down. It's a little bit more strategic. As the old saying goes, "Keep your friends close and your enemies closer."

It helps sometimes to have those little conversations that are not quite as confrontational. For example, if someone else down the table is talking, you could say to the person beside you (the one you have tension with), "It drives me crazy when people do that."

Now, what you're nicely saying is, "When you do that, it bothers me." But you're saying it in a very inoffensive way.

Stage Three

The stage three level of conflict is hopefully a level of conflict that doesn't happen very often at work, although it definitely happens in our personal lives. The third level really is the battle. That's when the conflict or the tension has turned to very black-and-white thinking. It builds from someone just needing to win to not only needing to win, but to hurt you in the process. When things reach this point the other person is saying,

"Winning for me is not enough. I need to take you down." You see a lot of this in sports. Let's take a hockey example.

Team A and Team B have reached round one of the playoffs and it's a best-of-seven series. By game three, Team B has won three games, so they just need one more game to win.

Team A realizes they're not likely to win the series, so their goal changes from winning to hurting Team A. The thought process changes to, "If we can't win, we don't want you to win either."

There was a case in the National Football League where a team was actually fined because they were paying players extra for intentionally hurting players on the other team. Same thing. Level three is when the tension is out of control.

When we reach the third level of conflict, logic and reason disappear and it's simply a battle.

You might not think you're in the third level of conflict. You might not be in that battle zone, but the person that you're having tension with is absolutely there, and it's their goal to not only win, but to take you down in the process. Your approach is to sit down and figure out the problem like adults, but if the other person is in battle mode it won't necessarily happen that way.

Divorce is a great example of that as well. You can have a couple arguing over every dime, and they're losing the kids in the conversation. They just want to bleed each other dry. "I'm not getting the house, but neither are you." They forget that the kids have to live somewhere, so where's the logic in that? There's no logic, because they're in the third level of conflict.

When you realize you're in the third level of conflict, you need to minimize your losses. You need to remove yourself from that situation, and prepare to refocus. You need a cooling-off period, because you can't deal with the confrontation when the emotions are that high. You're just not going to say and do the right thing; you need to get out.

When you're dealing with someone at that level, or if you are at that level, you almost always need negotiation and arbitration. Whether that's your union or your Human Resources department, you need that third party to be in the middle.

Of course in order for that third party to come into the situation, both sides have to be willing. There are many union situations, for example, where neither side is open to that arbitration. They want to battle it out. Some type of intervention team is necessary but both parties are not always willing (remember, logic and reason are gone at this point).

The challenge with this battle stage is that when people are locked into this final level of conflict, they often prolong it even after the arbitration is over. So even when it's been fixed — it's not fixed.

When I'm coaching people in a difficult work situation, and they've reached this level, I usually say, "Quite frankly, you need to find another job, because there's no happy answer at the end of this."

You certainly see third level conflict in personal relationships, and when that's the case, the relationship is usually over. You have no more contact with that person.

It can even happen with a client in a company, and that's why many companies will "fire" clients. They don't want to do business with those clients any more.

If the conflict, at level three, is with a coworker, one of you has to leave. There is no happily ever after here and rarely even tolerance. And besides, shouldn't work be somewhere you like to spend your time – not somewhere you are hating every second?

I would like to think that you will never actually face this situation in the workplace. The reality is that typically one of the two involved will leave before it gets to this point. Not always, but if I were in the situation, I would do my best to work it out on levels one and two and if they made it to level three, I would be so unhappy I would immediately start looking for another job. My sanity is worth more than a job to me.

You have to have a confrontation here. You have to say what needs to be said and you have to fix it the best you can, but then in the end you have to get out.

Those are the three stages. They don't necessarily follow any pattern. It would be nice if they always went from one to two to three, but they don't always do that. Some situations start immediately in level three. Most of them start in level one. Level one is often fixed with a conversation and can be fairly innocuous. Not a big deal and the tension can be removed easily just by bringing it to the other person's attention.

It's in level two that confrontation really starts, and that can be the turning point as to whether it escalates up to level three or whether it's fixed.

Chapter Three: Reactions

One of the activities that I use in my "Dealing with Difficult People" program (and I talk about it in that book as well) is the "pattycake" exercise. Here's how it works:

First, I put everyone in pairs and ask them to imagine they are playing the childhood game of pattycake. Standing up and facing each other, they put their hands against their partners' hands.

In each pair there is a Partner A and a Partner B and we quickly assign roles. I give the following instructions very quickly:

On the count of three, I want Partner A to push as hard as possible on Partner B.

1-2-3 Go! Of course, Partner A pushes as hard as possible, which is exactly what I told them to do. Note, I don't tell Partner B what to do at all. After just a few seconds I tell them to stop. Then I'll say, "Partner A, congratulations. You did what you're supposed to do. You've earned a raise. You followed instructions well and you're getting a promotion! Partner B, I didn't tell you what to do. What did you do?"

You know that every single Partner B pushed back! It's an instinctive reaction that when somebody pushes us, we feel threatened (literally and figuratively). When we feel threatened we push back. Here's how the conversation goes:

Me:	So, Partner B, why did you push back? You weren't told to push back.
Partner B:	It was instinctive I pushed automatically without thinking about it.
	back, what did you do?
Partner A:	I pushed even harder.
Me:	Partner A, you were trying to do your job and it seemed like Partner B was being difficult, right?
Partner A:	Yeah, absolutely. They were stopping me from doing what I was trying to do.
Me:	Partner B, why did you push back? Did Partner A seem difficult?
Partner B:	Yeah, they were trying to knock me over.
Me:	Partner A, were you trying to knock Partner B over?
Partner A:	(usually laughing) No – just pushing hard. Not trying to hurt, just following instructions.
Me:	Partner B wasn't Partner A just trying to do their job?
Partner B:	Well, it didn't feel that way.

The reality is that all conflict relationships—all difficult people relationships — involve two people. Conflict is not a one-person experience. There's always reaction. Now, much of the time, the reaction is innocent. They don't realize that they're doing something that is wrong from the other person's standpoint.

Whenever your psychological need has been violated, you're going to react, and your reaction is going to cause a reaction on the other person, and vice versa. There are four ways we react when a psychological need is violated.

Retaliation

The first way is retaliation. That is, "Don't get mad, get even." "What goes around comes around." When someone cuts you off on the highway, do you cut them off in return? When you are driving down the highway and someone tail gates you and flashes their lights, do you slow down? Do you tap the breaks? All of that is retaliation.

At the workplace, if someone takes the last cup of coffee, instead of making a full pot, do you make just one cup? "Fine. You're not making coffee for me? I'm not making coffee for you."

It's passive-aggressive, but many people don't realize they are being passive-aggressive when they do that. They just say, "Oh, I'll show you that you're being a jerk." But really, you're being a jerk back, aren't you?

That's part of the problem, because by responding in kind you're escalating the tension, because you think it's not fair. It's not fair they're driving into my bumper and making it dangerous on the road for me. It's not fair they took the last cup of coffee and didn't make more. It's not fair they always leave early and I am not able to. So because you think it's not fair, your needs are violated. So you react in a very passive-aggressive way by pushing back (retaliating).

Domination

Another way of reacting is the dominating reaction. This reaction is not passive-aggressive — it's just plain aggressive. That's the bully approach: my way or else. And in the workplace, that usually happens when someone has a little bit of authority behind their name and title.

"I don't see why we need to create this report." "Because I said so. Because I'm the boss of you." "Because I want it. It doesn't matter. You're not paid to think." The dominating style is very hard on relationships long-term, but what I find fascinating is that's how we parent.

That's how we actually teach children — who, of course, become adults — how to deal with authority. It's a parenting style. I'm not talking about whether it's right or wrong, but I have children (adults now) and I have to admit I did it too.

"Eat all your vegetables or you don't get dessert." "Do your homework or you can't go outside and play." It becomes a "because I said so" approach.

It's also an old style of management. If you have worked in a very traditional organization where there's a very clear hierarchy, and it's a "yes, sir" type approach, that might be how you handle pushback. When someone asks "why?", when someone challenges why you're doing things, "Because I said so" might be your reaction style.

Think about it. Are you in that very traditional hierarchy frame of mind? If you are, you're actually contributing to a lot of tension without realizing it. You think you're due respect, but the other person isn't so sure.

Your psychological need — the need to be valued, which is respect, has been violated when someone questions you. "Why do I need to do this?" "Well, it's not up to you to ask why." That's a dominating reaction.

Suppression

The most common reaction, and usually the reason people need confrontation skills in the first place, is the reaction we call suppressing. We could also call it ignoring it or justifying it.

The person justifies the situation. They ignore the situation. They talk themselves out of any conversation or confrontation. They isolate the situation. They don't respond at the time because they don't know what, how, when, or where to say the right thing.

Then, twenty minutes later, or an hour later, they think, "It's no big deal." They talk themselves out of it, because the need to avoid confrontation is so high that they accept it and let it go.

They think, "It'll go away. It's no big deal. Yes, they left the coffee pot empty. They must have been in a hurry." Well, they must be in a hurry every single time they go to the coffee pot, mustn't they? And they justify the behavior instead of addressing it.

Unfortunately, this is where the tension can build. You take that first level of conflict that we talked about — the little everyday stuff — and you justify: "Oh, they're busy," "Oh, they didn't even notice that the photocopier was jammed," "Oh, they think that the cleaning staff runs the dishwasher."

By not saying anything, you're saying it's okay. In your head it's not okay, but as far as they're concerned, it is.

Let's use a personal example. If you live in a condo, and someone always parks in your parking spot, and you never leave a little note, and you never say to them, "That's my parking spot," you've given them tacit permission to park there.

Then one day you call up a tow truck company, and you say, "Get that car out of there!" and you've put up a great big aggressive sign that says, "This spot is not for you!" That's a huge overreaction that the other person never even saw coming. From their perspective, they were allowed to park there. No-one told them otherwise.

Co-operation

The fourth reaction is the one we really want, and that's co-operation. We work together, we discuss the problem and we co-operate in finding the solution.

In theory that's where we all want to go, but the problem is the comfort zone. For most of us, saying something to the other person takes us out of our comfort zone and we're afraid of potential consequences. Because of that, we rarely make it to the co-operation stage.

This goes to the nub of what we're doing wrong. We're part of the problem because we're overreacting, we're being passive-aggressive or aggressive, or we're ignoring. What we need to do instead is be part of the solution by cooperating and having the confrontation in a healthy manner.

Chapter Four: Conflict Management Styles

There are five different styles of conflict management, and the reality is not one approach will work in all situations. We need to master all the styles and decide which is the right solution is for each situation.

So let's look in some detail at the five styles.

Collaborating

The first style of conflict management is called the Collaborating style, and it works very well when we're in Stage One of conflict. This is where it isn't personal. It's a win/win style of conflict management. It works well when we're dealing departmentally. It works well with kids, with family. It's a problem-solving style of conflict management.

In the collaborating style, we're exchanging information. We're saying, "This is what I want and this is what you want" and everybody reaches a solution that's acceptable.

It's not compromise, because neither party has to give in. It's, "Oh, I didn't know that" or "Let's try this" or "Oh yes, that makes sense." It really is about finding a solution that works well for everyone, unlike compromise which often satisfies no one.

There are limitations to the collaborating style. For instance, it's not effective when someone lacks commitment and they're not interested in working with you. It's not effective when someone is in Stage Three of conflict, where there's no logic being used. It's not effective where time is limited.

It is effective, however, where we're really trying to, as a group of people — a department or a family — work well together to get a solution that pleases everyone. In a family situation, for example, we all go to the Red Box to pick what movie we want to watch. It's not that it's your turn to pick. It's, "Let's find a movie everyone wants to watch." We may go through twenty movies until everyone says, "Yes!" and we've found one that one that makes everybody happy. That's what collaboration is.

At work, it could be dealing with vacation schedules or flex work time.

It could be seating arrangements in the office. If we just say, "You sit here. You sit here. You sit here," no one's happy. Try instead, "Where do you want to sit? Great, because I want to sit here." Perfect. Everybody's happy. That's collaboration.

Compromise would be "You sit by the window, and then I get early lunch". We both want the window and we both want early lunch, so with compromise we each give in a little bit. Compromise is giving in a little. Collaboration, on the other hand, doesn't require you to give. Each person gets what they wanted. Many times all it takes is a conversation and you can easily achieve collaboration (if everyone is willing of course, which isn't always the case).

Dominating

The Dominating style of conflict management is defined as a person who has high concern for him or herself and virtually no concern for the other person. Of course it's the bullying style. As you can imagine, we shouldn't be using this style professionally very often at all. It's really emphasis on me, on self. It's only used when you have authority. It's intimidation.

You could use it in high-cost situations, in parenting situations, in legal regulation situations. Somebody says, for example, "When you're driving the company vehicle, you cannot have your cellphone on at all." The other person says, "I need it for my kids, if my kids are in an emergency." But the response is, "If your cell phone is on, you're going to lose your job."

Only in very rare situations is it completely black and white, not just because you're the boss, but because there's some very compelling reason why something needs to be done. When the fire alarm goes, you're not allowed to grab your laptop and bring it with you. Leave it behind and get out of the building. The domination style is justified here because it is a safety situation.

As you can imagine, we're going to virtually never need that in a normal work situation. If you go back to where I talk about how we mishandle confrontation, one of the things that we're often doing wrong in tension-filled situations is taking that dominating style.

You have to do a real examination of your own style. Are you moving into that dominating style when you shouldn't be? Are you trying to use the wrong tool for the job? While that is a conflict management style, it should not be your norm — not even close to your norm. It should be a very rare occasion that you would use this style. If you can evaluate yourself and say, "Yes, I use that one every once in a while," I want you to look back and say, "How's that working for you?" Because it's probably not.

Postponing

Probably the most effective conflict management style is called Postponing. What postponing does, is it takes the situation as it's happening, and allows you to get back in control.

Right now, there is a situation unfolding in front of you. There's a conflict happening, and you don't have your strategy in place. You're not ready or prepared to handle it. Instead of saying something wrong, or instead of isolating, suppressing or ignoring, what you're going to do is use an assertive technique to get you through that moment, to calm the moment down. Then, within the next 24 hours, you're actually going to have a confrontation.

When something happens, you have a 24hour window in which to deal with it. If you let it continue past the 24 hours, it seems to the other person that you've given permission for this behaviour. So let's go back to that situation where I come to the meeting late because I was in a conference call, and someone says, "About time you got here. Sorry, did we interrupt your nap time?" That is the wrong place for me to have this confrontation. I will lose that confrontation at that point.

So instead, I will choose the postponing style. I'll use one of the assertive techniques we'll talk about in an upcoming chapter, and then, within the next 24 hours, I will approach Bob privately, and I'll say, "Bob, I'd like to talk to you about what happened at the meeting this afternoon."

I don't have to talk to him now, but I have to schedule to talk within 24 hours. Say, "Tomorrow, let's go to the coffee shop at 10:30. I'll buy you a coffee. I want to talk privately."

Because I've brought it to his attention, he knows what's coming. He's not caught by surprise. I'm not going to bully him into having the confrontation on my terms only; I'm going to cooperate and have the conversation at a mutually agreeable time. By bringing it to his attention within 24 hours, I've taken away the permission for this behavior. I am going to have the confrontation, but when it's under my control, when I can figure out what I'm going to say, and I have all my tools in my toolkit ready to go.

The postponing really is buying me time. It's saying, "I'm going to deal with it in my time frame." That really is what you want to do. I find this one of the most successful styles because it allows me to be in control, and be strategic about what I want to say.

There is one caveat though. Sometimes people think they're postponing, and then within a few hours, they think, "It was no big deal. I overreacted." With that, they go back to giving permission. So while postponing is a really good style of conflict management, you need to make sure you're not giving yourself permission to back down. Don't allow the suppressing style of reacting to take over.

Giving In

The fourth style of conflict management is Giving In. There are times when the best way to handle tension is to let it happen without a reaction. That's a strategic choice you make because you put a higher value on the relationship than you do on the situation.

If it's my coworker who's always leaving the coffee pot empty, that relationship may or may not be that important to me. But if it's my boss who's always leaving the coffeepot empty, that relationship is probably more important, and I'm more likely to ignore the behaviour. Maybe.

The giving in style is usually used more in your personal life. With your partner, with your mother-in-law, with your relatives. That's because the relationship is really far more important than the individual situation.

At work, there are some relationships that are important enough to give in, but ask yourself if you are really giving yourself permission to ignore things or not?

You must decide whether or not you're willing to give something up for the relationship. That means you've got to give up the tension. It has to stop bothering you. If it is still bothering you, then you didn't give it up.

In the silly old coffee example, that means that every time you go to the coffeepot and you see that it's empty, you can't say, "Oh, I know who left that empty." If you do that, you haven't really given it up.

You have to accept that this is going to continue, and decide you won't let it get under your skin. If you can't do that, then this is not the right style of conflict management for the situation, so you need to do something else.

My husband and I are in the midst of planning a golf tournament as a fundraiser to help raise money for the Ride to Conquer Cancer. Warren (my hubby) has to raise $2500. We have two other people on the team, Gael and Derrick, who also have to raise $2500 each.

At this point the golf tournament is three weeks away, and Gael and Derrick have done nothing to help support it. So far, Warren and I have done all the work. We've gathered all the teams, organized with the golf course, gathered sponsors and prizes. And, as you can imagine, it bothers us that we are the only ones doing all the work.

Gael and Derrick are very good friends of ours, and I'd like them to stay that way. I have taken a passive approach to reminding them of all the things that still need to be done for the tournament. They are aware they've done nothing. We will continue to do all the work for the tournament, and not have a conversation about them doing nothing, yet reaping the rewards of our hard work. We won't have this conversation and it will not damage our friendship because the friendship means more to me than the work involved in the golf tournament. So we are giving in because the long-term relationship is more important than the short term work.

At work you may have a co-worker that is perpetually late for work, and you end up having to answer the phones or do part of her job. Is that five minutes each day important enough for you to have a conversation about it, or just not worth the tension it will cause? Now if you are giving up, you have to be sure to let go of the tension it is causing as well. Just because you agree not to say anything doesn't mean you've let it go. Be sure to let it go.

Compromise

The final style of conflict management is Compromise. Now, this is, again, what everyone thinks they want to do, but both sides have to be willing to compromise. And a lot of the time, both sides are not even close to willing to compromise.

Imagine two coworkers like to listen to different music. They work close together, in the same space. One of them likes heavy metal and one of them likes classical opera — opposite ends of the musical spectrum.

Is a compromise of listening to heavy metal in the morning and classical opera in the afternoon really a solution? No, because no one is really happy with that solution. Ideally they could work with the collaboration style and find a type of music they both enjoy (which isn't likely to happen in this example). But if they want to work harmoniously together, this might be the best option. Not ideal, but a solution nonetheless.

Compromise is powerful when both sides are right, but it is really quite a challenge when one side is clearly wrong. It's most effective when there's a balance of power — coworkers or peers, as opposed to the boss and an employee.

Everyone has to be willing to give something up to get to the resolution. So it's not collaborating, where we find an agreeable solution. We're both losing here. It's not entirely a win/ win. In fact, it's a little bit of a lose/lose.

There can be a win/win in there, but there's also a lose/lose — so it's really a win/lose. You see it in politics all the time. And who's happy at the end of the compromise, really? No one.

Growing up with my younger brother we were taught to compromise. "You watch your television show for half an hour, and I'll watch my television show for half an hour." When yours is on, I hate it. When mine is on, you hate it.

What kind of solution is that?

In the workplace, we think we're supposed to compromise all the time. That we have to give, give, give. It's not always the best kind of conflict management, because it leaves residual tension.

Obviously we want to be able to pick the style that is right for the right situation, where there is no residual tension. And if there is still some tension, you really didn't pick the best solution.

There isn't always a perfect fix to the tension, but you should always try to alleviate it somehow. Ignoring it certainly doesn't fix the situation, so pick the right strategy, based on the relationship, the severity of the situation, and the end result you desire.

In the next chapter we will discuss how to handle the situation in the moment. We won't always be able to think it through and pick the right solution in the moment. We need some emergency tools to handle the situation so that we can go back and clarify and plan our strategy.

Chapter Five: Assertive Responses

Assertive responses are behaviours that will handle even the most stressful situations or conflicts.

They're assertive in the moment so you can buy time to use that style of conflict management called postponing. They allow you to handle the moment without escalating it, and without giving permission. Instead of having your mind go blank and being able to say the "right" thing, implement one of these strategies so you can handle the surprise, get your control back and pick the right approach from the previous chapter.

The challenge with dealing with the confrontation on the spot, or in the moment is that you are actually likely to lose the confrontation, and potentially the respect of anyone who witnessed it. I know that I'm brilliant at three in the morning at coming up with the perfect response (which wake me up saying "Oh, I should have said....".) I'm not quite as talented when it happens at three in the afternoon!

Let's go back to that situation where I come into the meeting late because I'm on a conference call with a client, and Bob says, "About time you got here. Did we interrupt your nap time?"

I might be strongly tempted to look at him and say, "Don't be an idiot" or some other little smart comment, just to flip it off — telling him he's being a jerk. Or I might say, "Bob, I wasn't napping. Why are you always so sarcastic?"

But if I did that (as tempting as it may be), Bob (and maybe the others around the table) might have the reaction, "Rhonda, relax! I was just joking." Everyone is uncomfortable, everyone will say you over-reacted, and you lose. Bizarre reality, but it is true.

When Bob says, "Did we interrupt your nap time?" everyone will agree he's being a jerk. But as soon as I step down to his level, I'm a bigger jerk. You have to always be conscious of your timing. That's a big part of confrontation skills and in this situation, with a room full of people, the timing is off.

Whenever he says something offensive, I need to do something to tell him clearly that this is not okay. What I don't need to do is lash back, because I'm going to lose that battle every single time.

"Don't ever wrestle with a pig. You'll both get dirty, but the pig will enjoy it!"
—Cale Yarborough

So what do I mean by "do something"? Well, that something is an assertive response, and there are many to choose from.

Pick Your Strategy

The first and main overriding tip to handling

situations in the moment is, as Stephen Covey says, "Begin with the end in mind." What are you trying to do here? What is your overriding goal?

My strategy, for example, might be that when I'm with Bob, my goal is to keep my mouth shut. My goal is to not stoop down to his level.

I need to know what my overriding goal is all the time with Bob. When he says something like that — "Did we interrupt your nap time?" — my goal is to not be baited, to not play his game.

There's tension in our relationship, so I know that as soon as I walk through those doors, he's going to be there. I can give myself a little mental reminder: "Note to self: Rhonda, don't take the bait. Don't go there. Keep your mouth shut, whatever he says or does." See what I mean? That's a main, overriding, in-the-moment know-what-your-goal-is strategy.

"Don't take the bait" is a pretty big goal, because when someone is trying to bait you, you know they want to fight. They're good at it. They're verbally strong. They think they're being funny. They're drawing attention to themselves, and it's at your expense. If you're not willing to have that happen — and you shouldn't — you need an assertive response.

I won't always know a confrontation is coming. I always know that my strategy is to not fight back, not get baited, and not do anything that I will regret. Even with a stranger, that is my strategy. At a basic level, I know that I want to be in control in my confrontations, and in the moment, I am often not in control at all.

Don't Interrupt

There are times when the situation flies out of control quickly, and tempers flare up. If you have someone yelling at you, or berating you for whatever reason, be sure not to interrupt them.

When you interrupt someone when they are on a "rant" you are actually prolonging it. They will stop, the anger level will increase, and they will start all over.

For more information on dealing with difficult people and angry people, check out our companion book "Dealing with Difficult People" Chapter 9.

Camouflage

One of the easiest techniques is called camouflage. When I was a kid, I used to play with Barbie and the other dolls like her. You had Barbie, and then there was GI Joe. GI Joe always came in the camouflage outfit. The reason he was dressed in camouflage was so he could be in the jungle and Barbie couldn't find him. You need to hide in the jungle from the person who is trying to get (or bait) you as well.

You need to have your camouflage outfit. This means disguising the situation so it looks like you don't see the attack the person is delivering. You use the camouflage when someone is behaving inappropriately. You want to handle the situation without getting into the confrontation, at that point, because it isn't the right time.

Let's say I'm choosing the postpone method of conflict management. When Bob says to me, "Did we interrupt your nap time?", a camouflage might be for me to look at the entire room and say, "I apologize for being five minutes late. I was on a conference call with ABC client."

I can still see in the jungle, and see that Bob is staging an attack (by me being the butt of his joke). I'm not going to address him directly – I am disguising my response to almost look naïve. I'm not taking his bait, I'm not laughing at his joke. However, I did see the comment was about me being late, so I'm camouflaging the real issue (Bob being a jerk) and addressing the issue to everyone (not attacking Bob back). I've not completely ignored it. I just covered it up. I would say that to everyone. I'm ignoring his comment, but I'm addressing the content of his comment. I'm addressing the issue instead of his comment.

The Look

The next assertive response is actually one of my favourites, because I'm a parent, and all parents know how to give the look. When you use the look as a response, you make prolonged eye contact with somebody, but about four seconds too long. And the look says, "If looks could kill, you'd be dead right now." You actually say nothing.

I've said and done nothing, but I certainly have not given permission for the behaviour. So when Bob says, "Did we interrupt your nap time?", I make eye contact with him for four seconds too long — which is a really long time. Then everybody in the room gets the message I'm sending Bob. I didn't do anything to step out of line, but the look said, "Don't do that."

I don't suggest you do it all the time. It's as if you're saying, "We're going to talk about this later. You and I will chat privately." Spouses do that all the time, don't they?

When you use the look, everyone knows what is happening. It's clear that you've handled the situation in the moment; you're just not escalating it in front of everyone. You're going to get your ducks in a row so that you know exactly what you're going to say a little later on.

And since the look is so noticeable, Bob knows that you are going to confront him later (or he will learn it very quickly), and soon he will stop attacking you in public because he will want to avoid that confrontation.

Everyone hates confrontation. Even Bob. Bob is trying to be funny, attack you without doing anything you can accuse him of. He does it in public because it is "safe". He doesn't want you to confront him as he is uncomfortable too. If you start getting a little more comfortable with confronting Bob, you might find his behaviour changes quickly.

Ignore it

It sometimes is that easy. Pretend you didn't hear the comment, don't react to it, and keep on going. It is pretty much a non-response. You appear as if you are completely naïve to what was just said or done, but you are not.

You are still going to deal with the offender at a later date, if possible.

Or not. It depends on the situation and your strategy.

A few years ago, I was driving on the parkway in my town, when I was confronted by my first experience with road rage. I wasn't prepared for it, and really was just paralyzed by the situation.

I merged onto the parkway, at what I felt was a safe speed and comfortable distance in front of the car behind me. Clearly, the man in the car behind me did not agree.

A short way up the road the traffic was bumper to bumper and everyone was stopped. I wasn't looking out my rear view mirror (we were stopped after all), so I didn't see the man get out of his car and approach mine until he knocked on my window.

I was completely shocked, and did a dumb thing. I rolled down the window (I really do know better, but I was completely taken off guard, and I'm not perfect).

The man proceeded to rip a strip off me about my driving, and safety etc.

I had recovered enough to know not to engage him in debate. This was one confrontation I was not going to have (sometimes your safety needs to win over your pride). Pick your battles after all, and I chose not to fight this one.

I didn't interrupt him, I didn't do anything while he was venting. I kept a straight face, kept eye-contact, and I listened to him.

When he was done, I said that I hoped he had a nice day, and I rolled up my window.

I completely ignored his tirade. I didn't defend my actions, I pretended I hadn't even heard them.
That was the right answer too. Then I laughed all the way down the road as he had gotten so upset, and I had not.

Always In Private

Always, always, always have your confrontation, your conversation, in private. You never, ever have it in front of other people.

The conference room is not private (unless the door is closed and no one else is in the room). A cubicle is not private. Even the washroom in the office is not private. So in public situations where conflict happens, where there are other people around, always take the high road and don't handle the situation right there.

You might be prepared to handle it right there, but don't. By using this assertive response, you are respectful of your own needs and of other people's needs. Always have these conversations and confrontations away from the eyes and ears of others.

The Broken Record

Another approach is called the broken record technique, which is very useful if you are in a customer service role and you are often dealing with people on the phone. You don't know who the person on the other end of the line is. It's not as if you can say, "Can we finish this conversation later?" Sometimes you just have to handle it in the moment.

Obviously you can't give the look on the phone. You can, however, do the broken record technique, and that's the one that I suggest when the other person just wants to have the confrontation now.

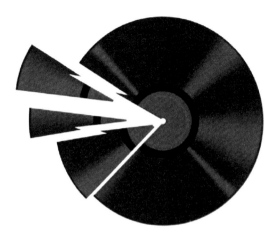

They're ready. They're good to go, and you're not. You didn't see it coming. You didn't know. You're not prepared, but you're only going to get one shot at this confrontation because the situation doesn't allow for it to be postponed.

The broken record technique might sound like this:

Customer:	I want my repairs done for free. You messed up and now you need to fix it. I'm not paying for it.
Rhonda:	Unfortunately sir, our investigation indicates that it was user error, and you are responsible for the repair charges.
Customer:	No way! I am not paying for it. I didn't do anything to it!
Rhonda:	Unfortunately sir, our investigation indicates that it was user error and you are responsible for the repair charges.
OR	
Mary:	Rhonda, We need to talk to you about blah blah blah blah blah.
Me:	This is not a good time for me. Could we have this conversation at two o'clock?
Mary:	No, I need to talk about it now.
Me:	This is not a good time for me. Can we have this conversation at two o'clock?

You think of one of those little lines, such as "This is not a good time for me", which is actually a very good opening. Then you figure out how you want to finish it. What's nice about the broken record technique is you never run out of things to say!

Don't change the words. Say exactly the same thing in a nice calm voice. Don't paraphrase it, don't adjust the message. Repeat yourself as necessary.

It makes you aggressive. You are definitely being aggressive.

But after all, you're dealing with an aggressive person. They are insisting on having a conversation now, and now's not a good time for you. It's, again, one of those almost bully techniques that you would use in very few situations, but there are times when it's exactly what you need to do.

Imagine you were in a driving accident with another driver, and the other person is instantly at full-blown stage three conflict. They're yelling and screaming at you for being a stupid driver, being totally unrealistic, and you're thinking, "Man, I don't want to get into this right now. This is a bad place."

They say, "Get out of this car. We need to talk." Using the broken record technique, you say "I'm staying here till the police arrive." You just stick with that line. It's not as if you can say, "Can we talk about this tomorrow?" So it really is in a high-pressure sort of stage three-type situation and you need to get yourself prepared.

"I" Language

Always use "I" language. "I want," "I think," "I feel," or, "I need," as opposed to, "you should," "you have to," "you need to," "you must." Using "I" language is being respectful, and that's important.

Keep in mind that using "I" language in this situation is not "me, me, me" language. You don't dominate the conversation talking about yourself. It isn't a narcissistic approach to communication, but rather a non-defensive one.

Any sentence that starts with the word "you" — even if you have really good intentions — just has so much potential to go wrong. If your sentence that starts with the word "you" , then it immediately creates a defensive reaction – even when there is no tension in the relationship. When there is tension in the relationship, it is far worse!

Think at home how "I need you to empty out the dishwasher" sounds better than "You need to empty out the dishwasher". It really is saying the same thing, but it is heard and understood very differently.

"You need to watch what you say to me in public" sounds far more intimidating than, "I was uncomfortable with what was said yesterday." It's really the same message, but it's the way that it's perceived that changes the tone. Using "I" language is a way to be assertive while still taking the high road.

> "I've taken the high road so many times I have nosebleeds!"
> — *Marion Grobb Finkelstein*

You don't get a chance to have this confrontation again, so don't regret how or what you said to someone. Make sure you're always doing the right thing.

Always make it clear what you want from the situation. Remember earlier I said "Begin with the end in mind"? As often as possible, create that strategy, and know what your 'end in mind', or your intent, is. When you know what it is that you want to do, say and avoid, it makes handling the situation much easier because you aren't really caught off guard.

There are times when you will be completely gob smacked when something happens. Always have the look, ignore or camouflage in your toolkit so you can pull them out as needed, without warning.

When it is time to have my confrontation with Bob, for example, I can say "I would appreciate it if, when I come into meetings late, you don't acknowledge that I'm late. I will apologize. It isn't necessary to bring it to anyone's attention."

Give them examples of the behaviour you're looking for. "I would appreciate it if whoever takes the last cup of coffee makes another pot. Then there will always be some for the next person."

Tell people what to do. It sounds really basic, but people are not mind readers and they don't necessarily understand what you're upset about. They often don't agree that you should be upset either. Bob was just making a joke about me being late — why should I be upset? But, I am, so I need to tell Bob what is okay and what is not okay for me. Give examples.

If you say, for example, "I can't believe nobody cleans up this office! I'm the only one that cleans up!", that may not be clear to others. What do you mean by "clean up"? Do you mean run the dishwasher? Do you mean put the dishes in the sink? Because in my world, that's "cleaned up." If in your world, it means putting the dishes in the dishwasher and switching it on, you need to say so.

Ask a Question

To be assertive in those tension-filled moments, it takes few words. The more passive we become, the more words we use. We try to explain. We try to justify. Just be short and sweet. Always be polite and respectful and try to take that high road.

I have a secret weapon for when I'm in a critical moment and I'm scrambling in my mind about what to say: I ask a question and then stop talking.

If someone were to say, for example, "You never do this for me," you might say, "Could you explain?" "Could you give me an example?" Then zip it. Often people have a hard time with confrontation, because they don't know when to shut up.

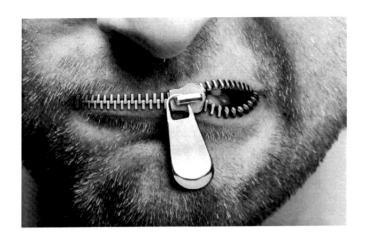

That is actually one of the biggest secrets of dealing with very high-tension-filled situations — just learn to stop talking. And that is certainly something that makes a huge difference in how much information you get, how much understanding you get, and how well you handle the situation.

We talk too much, so let's talk less!

Chapter Six: Controlling Your Emotions

Being emotional in confrontation is completely normal. That's especially true at the second stage, where the situation become personal. If your emotions are not engaged at that point, I'd be surprised.

Everybody's emotions are engaged. They pretty much show themselves in one of three ways. Some people cry, some people yell and some people blank out. Those are pretty much all the options — although some people do all three!

Knowing that they're going to be emotional is the reason people avoid confrontation.

You don't want to blank out. You don't want to wake up at three in the morning saying to yourself, "Oh, I should have said . . ." because you don't get a do-over!

You don't want to yell, because you know that that's really not the right answer.

You don't want to cry, because you think it makes you look weak.

I have several tips on emotional first-aid and keeping your emotions under control.

Eye Contact

The first tip is to maintain eye contact. The eyes are the window to the soul, and so the challenge with eye contact is that we pick up the other person's emotions. If someone is angry, we pick up on their anger. If someone is crying, we pick up on their crying.

However, you need to maintain eye contact. Lack of eye contact certainly can send the wrong message. It can unintentionally show disrespect. It could show fear. It could show condescension. There are so many things it could show, many of which are not what you want. So you need to maintain eye contact, even if just to avoid a misunderstanding.

My secret to maintaining eye contact in an emotional situation is to look right between their eyebrows. When you do this, it creates the illusion that you're making eye contact with that person, even though you're actually not.

That allows you to detach from their emotions. So you're not necessarily going to pick up their anger, their tears, and their emotions as well. Remind yourself to look right between the eyebrows, and that gives you a place to focus on.

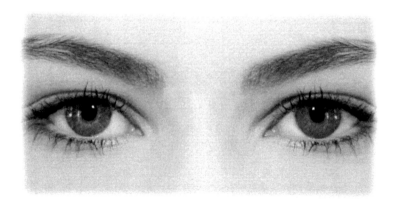

Note, if you practice this with a loved one, and you are nice and close to them, they will realize that you aren't making eye contact. If you are that close, close your eyes, and kiss.

Standing Up

If you can — and it won't be possible in all situations — one of the ways that you can control your emotions is through standing. You have better oxygen flow when you're standing, and you will get more oxygen to your brain while standing — which, of course, you need.

If you're on the telephone, that's easy to do. You just stand up. You're going to sound better. You're going to feel better. You're going to think better.

However, if you're sitting at a board room table and you stand, you're suddenly going to appear very aggressive. You have to be aware of the impression standing will create, and do this strategically.

For example, let's say I used Postponing by asking someone, "Can we go to coffee together tomorrow?" When we're standing in line at the coffee shop, this might be a good time to start this confrontation, as opposed to when we're sitting down in the coffee shop. It might be more comfortable to be standing.

We may never get to the table to sit, preferring to have the conversation standing. It will probably be a quick conversation, and it won't necessarily seem strange for you to have the entire conversation standing.

You control your emotions through the better oxygen flow standing gives you. If you start it standing, stay standing. If you're in the middle of the confrontation, you're not likely to be able to get up; but if you can, without it appearing aggressive, then stand during the confrontation. It allows you to control your emotions better.

The Toe Wiggle

Crying is one of those emotional responses that tends to be a little more female based, and it tends to annoy whoever is doing the crying, because that's the last thing they wanted to do. They want to hold it together, and they cry. I've got a couple of tips for when you're crying. (And by the way, I don't call it crying — I call it "eyes leaking"!)

When my eyes leak when I don't want them to, I wiggle my toes. If you were to wiggle your toes right now, you'd have to consciously think about it. You can't subconsciously wiggle your toes! What that does is distract your mind. Your mind is saying, "wiggle wiggle wiggle wiggle wiggle." While you are still hearing the other person speak, you're thinking, "You're right. I can't do that without thinking about it." It's a useful little bit of distraction.

Another bonus to the toe wiggle is that it relaxes your muscles. If you've ever had surgery and they need to give you a needle prior to it (especially if it is an intramuscular injection), they will tell you to wiggle your toes so you can't tense up your butt muscle. This avoids an adrenaline buildup in your muscles and you won't bruise. So it actually does relax you a little bit to wiggle your toes.

Now, the toe wiggle won't necessarily stop you from crying. What it does do is distract you a little bit. I do this at funerals. I sit there and I "wiggle wiggle wiggle." It's just is a muscle relaxant. It stops you from thinking "I'm crying and I don't want to cry", which often makes you cry more. It provides a little distraction, and keeps the tears from becoming a full out melt down of the "ugly cry" we certainly don't want to have.

By the way, as a side note, I also suggest you wiggle your toes in the middle of the night if you can't sleep, because you can't think about solving the world's problems when you're wiggling your toes! (wiggle, wiggle, wiggle!)

Push Up on the Septum

Another technique to try when you're crying is to take your index finger and push up on the septum of your nose — like when you try to stifle a sneeze. That will often reduce your reactions/tears as well.

Sometimes the tears will still leak out because they're sitting in your tear ducts, but it stops the gasping breaths, the really ugly cry. Just pushing up on the septum will sometimes allow you to hold your emotions in a little bit more as well.

Keep Going — and Don't Apologize

Another thing that I'll tell you to do when you're crying is to just keep going. Even if you cry, don't stop your confrontation. Even through the tears, keep moving towards your desired result.

Your crying is your body's fight or flight reaction, and it's trying to get out of the situation. You've taught it before that when you cry, the situation will go away. As soon as you start to cry, somebody will say, "Do you need a minute? Do you want to do this later?" Just say, "No, I want to keep on going." What will happen is you'll cry for about minute, and then all of a sudden you get your legs back. While the eyes still might be leaking a little bit, your voice will be better.

If you've ever had to give a eulogy at a funeral, that's a perfect example of how continuing on does make the situation better after about a minute. You cry for about the first minute of speaking. But obviously your eulogy is longer than one minute, so you get better as you show your body, "You're not getting out of this one."

When you are having a confrontation, and your eyes start to leak, don't acknowledge it. Don't apologize for it. If you need to, take a tissue and wipe the tears. Don't postpone the conversation. Keep on going, and you actually get better with time.

Not that you should get a lot of experience, but if you just keep showing your body, "It doesn't matter that you're crying. I'm going to do this anyway," it learns to stop crying. It's as if it learns to stop being embarrassed.

Lower the Volume

Are you more of a yeller than a crier? Then you'll find when you're in a confrontation, you'll yell even louder. What you really want to do is learn to lower the volume of your voice. Consciously speak a couple of levels quieter than your normal volume.

It's a little bit lower and a little bit softer. What you're actually doing is making the person listen more closely to you. It is possible they are not even listening to you at all (in which case it doesn't really matter what you do), but if they are, they have to work harder to hear what you're saying.

If you know that you're a yeller, consciously say to yourself, "Talk more softly. Lower the volume". As your voice becomes softer you will notice more of a normal volume, and voila! You're not yelling any more.

The same advice applies if the other person is yelling: talk softly. It actually shows the differences between the two levels. Lower your voice a little bit and hopefully they will pick up the cue and do the same (sub consciously of course).

Keep Still

Keep your hands still. If you need to, put them behind your back. Don't put them in your pocket and play with whatever's in your pocket. Don't fidget with a pen. Don't fidget with a paperclip or a piece of paper. Sit on your hands if you need to. You want to give the illusion of being very calm, and you can't do that if you're fidgeting.

The illusion is for yourself as well. If you start to fidget, your brain says, "Oh, I'm nervous now." You might blank out or have another nervous reaction because you've told your body you're nervous. Sit on your hands!

Write It Out

If you know you tend to blank out at the time of confrontation, there's absolutely nothing wrong with writing out what you want to say on paper. This isn't so you can email it to them, but it would be fine for you to print it out and bring it with you. If you want to read it, read it. Don't give it to them.

The reality is you won't read all of it. You'll start to read, and then you'll get comfortable with what you're going to say. This allows you to at least think about what you want to say beforehand, to get prepared. Instead of just reacting to the situation, you will be prepared and much more likely to keep to the point you are trying to make.

If blanking out is your issue, then practicing beforehand is your answer. If you're going to go into this confrontation with a specific intention, you should be prepared with what you're going to say. Practice beforehand.

Watch Your Self-Talk

Watch for and be aware of your emotions. Watch all the things that you say to yourself. If you say, "Now, don't yell. Don't cry. Don't blank out," you're telling your subconscious mind to yell, cry, and blank out. The subconscious mind doesn't understand the verb "don't." It only understands action verbs. It hears "do."

If you say, "Don't cry, don't cry, don't cry," it hears, "Cry, cry, cry." Of course that's exactly what you're going to do. Turn it around and make it positive. Say, "Keep calm. Breathe deeply. Take your time." All very positive action words. That helps you stay more relaxed as well during pressure situations.

Focus on Behaviour

Focus on the behaviour, not the person. You don't want to focus on, "Bob's a jerk. Bob's . . . " You want to focus on what it is that Bob is doing. Bob is using me as the butt of his humour. I don't like it. I don't like being the butt of a joke. That's what the problem is. Bob's not the problem.

When we get emotional, it's because we've made the situation personal. We want to detach from the personal component and just look at behaviour.

Obviously there's a lot to keep in mind, but it's part of the strategy to keep yourself prepared to say what you need to say when you need to say it, and not allow yourself to blank out, to strain, or to cry.

Chapter Seven: Face-To-Face Confrontations

Preparation

You certainly want (and need) to be prepared as much as possible. If you follow my advice about setting your strategy and following it, you'll find that when you're having a confrontation it's usually scheduled. You want the other person to know that it's happening. You might have called them, or even sent them an email saying, "Can we go for coffee tomorrow at 2:00pm?", or, "Can I talk to you in an hour? I want to talk to you about something in private."

By scheduling it, you're not only getting yourself prepared, but you're also being respectful by letting the other person know that it's coming, so that they can be prepared too. You don't want to arrive at the scheduled meeting and have them say, "I have no idea what you're talking about." There's no need to ambush them. Just because others do it doesn't mean you should as well.

Before the confrontation, you're both aware that an uncomfortable conversation is going to happen. If it's a conversation, you don't necessarily need to make an appointment, because it's not filled with tension and there's not so much need for preparation.

You might casually say, "Oh, by the way, I noticed that X happened. Would you mind in the future . . . ?" They reply, "Oh, yes. Okay." It didn't feel threatening. So conversation is non-threatening and not nearly as stressful as a confrontation.

With a confrontation, though, you need to be prepared.

Is it Worth a Confrontation?

In deciding whether to have a confrontation, you need to ask yourself, "Am I blowing this out of proportion?" "When I bring this up to her, is it going to sound stupid?"

So am I going to have a confrontation about leaving the coffee pot empty? No, I'm not, because that's way over the top. There's no need for a confrontation for that. I may have a confrontation about the way they treat things in the office or the way they deal with other people's property, but not the coffee pot.

Am I blowing this completely out of proportion? Am I really looking at the real issue, or is it a cover for issues I have with the person? Is it really the coffee, or is it Mike? If I'm going to talk about the coffee, let's talk about the coffee, but let's not attack everything else.

It's similar to when couples get into arguments and one of them brings up stuff that happened six months earlier. That's not the issue. Before your confrontation, you need to know what the issue is.

Ask yourself whether their behavior — whatever it is that's causing tension in your life — is innocent or intentional. (I talk about this in some detail in Dealing with Difficult People.) Much of the time, people have behaviors that causes tension for you, but they are completely unaware that is causes tension for you.

If you're prepared to have a confrontation with that person, you need to ask yourself if the other person is even aware of what you are upset about. Is their behavior innocent or intentional? Are they doing this on purpose to bother you, or are they unaware it is a problem at all? Are you taking this way down a tension-filled path that it doesn't need to go down? Can you make this a whole lot easier?"

If you're really honest with yourself, and admit that they're unaware that this is a problem, then you're not likely going to have a confrontation with them. You're much more likely to have a conversation.

Can the Behaviour Be Changed?

Can their behavior change? Are you having a confrontation about something that's realistic to change?

As an example, assume that they are fidgeting constantly while at their desk. They don't sit still, and they drum their fingers on the table all the time. It drives you crazy. All day long, you just hear "drum drum drum drum drum."

One day, you've had enough of it, and you decide you're going to have a confrontation. Before you have your confrontation, ask yourself if they even know they're doing it. Is it innocent or intentional? Even if you bring it to their attention, can they change it? Maybe not.

Can someone change his or her accent? No. So even though you can't understand them in a meeting and that causes you a ton of tension, they can't change that. It's not possible.

Even if something really annoys you and causes huge amounts of frustration for you, it isn't smart to have a confrontation about something that the other person cannot or will not change.

Timing

Look at your timing before your confrontation. Most people like to have confrontations during Friday afternoons, so that they have the weekend to cool off and to think about it. Is that the best time? I'm not saying it's the worst time, but is that the best time?

Is Monday morning at nine o'clock the best time to have a confrontation? Probably not, because it might affect your entire week. Choose your time carefully.

The Battle vs the War

Will you win the battle and lose the war? Is this just a little piece of something much bigger? Recognize, especially in a workplace situation, that there are going to be consequences to a confrontation. Are you looking at what the consequences are?

If you have this confrontation, if you say, "I'm uncomfortable with X," there's going to be some type of spinoff. Have you looked at what the spinoff might potentially be, and are you prepared to live with that?

I had a situation where an employee had asked me for a raise. She came to me and said she wanted 25%. I said, "A 25% raise is not reasonable."

There was tension. There was conflict. We had the conversation.

I said, "Is this negotiable?" She said, "No." I said, "Well, then you need to find a job somewhere else that will pay you that amount, because it is too much."

She drew her line in the sand during our confrontation. She took a very dominant approach to conflict, said, "This is what I want. It's nonnegotiable." The consequence was she's looking for another job.

When I asked if her demand was negotiable, and she said 'no', did it occur to her that 'no' meant she was going to have to find another job? I don't think it did. It completely surprised her, because she hadn't considered in advance the possible consequences of the confrontation she chose to have.

We had a family situation some time ago where lots of family dynamics went wrong

— everybody was angry at somebody for something that had happened in the past.

When my father and his wife had a big 25th wedding anniversary, part of the fallout was that most of his family decided not to go to the party because they were angry with my brother.

They were expressing their anger at my brother, but unfortunately this meant they were not supporting my dad. They didn't see the consequence that my dad was the one to suffer.

Ever heard the expression "Cut off your nose to spite your face?" We have to look at consequences to ensure we aren't doing that. Tunnel vision on your issue will cause major consequences, so be sure to look carefully.

Third Party Arbitration

If you're going to bring in a third party because the situation has really escalated, it can't be one of your friends or co-workers. It must be someone impartial. It doesn't have to be the boss. The boss often doesn't want to have anything to do with the situation for fear of being caught in the middle.

Maybe it's HR. Maybe it's a union representative. Perhaps, it's another supervisor. It cannot

You:	Who else does it bother?
Me:	It doesn't matter who else it bothers. That's not the point.
You:	It matters to me who else it bothers.

be one of your friends or another coworker as that will feel like an ambush.

Avoid bringing other people into the situation. For example, if I complain about something you are doing and I say, "I'm not the only one it bothers you know," I have just brought other people into the situation, and that is a no-no.

As soon as I do that, I've derailed the situation. We're likely to have a conversation that goes like this:

I've derailed the conversation and I'm not likely to get the issue fixed because the problem is no longer the issue, the issue is who else it bothers.

You have to be very focused. Make sure you're really focusing on one issue and how that appears to you or affects you, what you think the potential collaboration is so you can both work together to find a solution. If necessary, find the compromise.

It takes a lot of thinking and preparation. Most people cannot handle confrontation spontaneously, and most people are just not logical enough about it in their thinking to be able to look at all of those things on the spur of the moment.

Even some casual conversations take a lot of prep work, and that's why people talk themselves out of them. They tell themselves it's too much effort. It's not too much effort. Don't talk yourself out of the conversation or confrontation; instead do the preparation if the confrontation or conversation is to be successful.

Chapter Eight: Danger Zones in Confrontation

Although we have covered exactly how to have a confrontation, there are a few "danger zones" during confrontations that we need to be aware of.

Calm Down

Probably the worst thing that you could ever say in a confrontation — the two worst possible words to say ever — are "calm down." Never, ever, ever tell anyone to calm down.

You may be perfectly calm, having mastered the art of confrontation in a professional manner. They may not be. Knowing that if a person just calmed down we would be able to have this confrontation far more effectively makes perfect sense to you. It doesn't to them.

It never works. If you don't believe me, try telling your spouse to calm down the next time he or she is upset. I bet you won't do it again!

Don't go prepared to tell them that they're blowing something out of proportion. Don't disregard their point of view. When you're doing your homework, hopefully you're looking at all possible ways that this confrontation could go.

It's NOT all about You

Most people, when having a confrontation, make it all about themselves. "This is what I want." "This is the way I see it." "This is what you're doing wrong." "This is what you need to do better." We really need to learn to not make it all about ourselves.

If you are prepared enough you should be able to see things from their perspective as well. Be balanced in your approach. If your confrontation sounds like it is all about what you want, the other person will react and make it all about what they want. That is a sure-fire no-win situation.

Private and Respectful

Always have your confrontations privately and respectfully. You don't ever want to regret what you said, especially in public.

Learn to Shut Up!

Make sure you're as strategic as possible.

Say little. Be effective with what you say. As I said earlier, stop talking! One of the big mistakes we make is just saying far too much.

The things that we do wrong happen because we become emotional. I don't mean crying or yelling, but getting carried away verbally. Learn to pull in the reins. Be strategic. Know what you want to say and then stop talking.

Chapter Nine: Steps to Follow and What to Say

While I'm not normally a fan of technique, I am going to teach you a technique in the form of steps that we'll follow in knowing exactly what to say. So far, we've talked about the strategy to get you to the confrontation. Now you'll learn to answer the question, "What are the words that I'm going to say?"

To help you remember, I'll use the word "desk," only I'll spell it differently: DESC.

Describe

"D" stands for describe; meaning describe the situation. Be objective, not subjective.

Describe it in black and white. Be very factual. Don't use your interpretation or your assumption. If Mike and I were in a meeting yesterday, and I was running the meeting, and I felt that Mike was fidgeting, tapping his pencil, yawning and obviously being very bored with the meeting, I would want to talk to him about this. It would be important to me because as a supervisor, I would assume that Mike is undermining my credibility.

I might say privately, "Mike, in yesterday's meeting, I noticed that you were really bored." However, that's very subjective. As soon as I say, "I noticed that you were bored," he's going to say, "No, no, no. I was up late last night with the baby" or something else that tells me I'm wrong. He could even say "No I wasn't". Then where do we go?

When I'm taking the first step — the D — I want his response to be, "Okay." I'm looking for a non-response, or something that shows he is wondering where I am going with this. I need to say something that's not going to cause any defensiveness on his part. I need to describe it in a way that's very factual.

Instead of saying, "Yesterday, Mike, I noticed that you were very bored," I might say, "Yesterday, Mike, I noticed you were tapping your pencil a lot during the meeting." What is his response going to be with that? I haven't accused him of anything. He is probably going to look at me strangely and say

"Ummm, okay" because he doesn't know where I'm going with this.

He's not likely to say, "No, I was up with the baby." That doesn't make sense, does it? What I need to say is something that gets a non-response. That is how to open up the conversation without immediately causing tension.

If I open the conversation with a statement that causes defensiveness, such as, "I noticed you were bored," all of a sudden the meeting has escalated. Instant tension. At that point we could go completely sideways, and we may not get to the point of what I'm trying to say at all.

My first comment is looking for a very bland response. "I noticed you were tapping your pencil on the desk." He's probably going to say, "Okay." I go to the next step now, because that "Okay" is what I was looking for.

Explain

"E" stands for explain.

Explain why this is a problem. Explain why it

causes an issue. Explain how it affects other people. It really does answer the question that Mike is wondering on where this is going because I'm now explaining why that was a problem.

We've described the situation, and now we're going to explain why it's a problem. Suppose I were to say, "I noticed you were tapping your pencil on the desk," and he replied, "Okay." I might then say, "The problem is, it made it look like you were bored." Notice, I'm not accusing him of being bored, because if I did that he would go on the defensive. I simply say, "It made it look like you were bored."

He might say, "No, I wasn't bored. I was up all night with the baby." I still need to get back to why it's a problem. "Now that I know you were up with the baby, I understand. But the problem is it took away my command of the room."

I've detached it. I've separated it emotionally from the explanation of what this behavior looks like to other people and why that is a problem.

They will still feel the need to defend themselves. Mike's still going to say, "I was up all night with the baby." I need to respond, "I'm sorry about that, but the reality is that this behaviour looks as if you are bored. I'm not saying you are. I'm saying this is what it looks like, and this is why it's a problem."

He is likely to still get defensive at this point, but we're not escalating tension.

Solution

"S" stands for solution.

This is in line with the strategy I spoke about earlier. Any time I'm going to have a confrontation with somebody, I need to know the end result I want. If I'm going to have a confrontation with Mike about his behavior in yesterday's meeting, I need to know the end result I'm looking for. Begin with the end in mind.

My end result might be simply that he doesn't do the pencil tapping at my meetings in future. I'll say something similar to, "Can I just ask you not to do that next time? Can I give you a sign to put the pencil down?" I'm nicely saying, "This is a problem. I know it's not a problem for you, but it's a problem for me and here is why it's a problem. And: "Here's what I think we should do."

Commitment

"C" stands for commitment.

You're basically going to get them to agree. "Yes, I'll do that. I think you're overreacting, but sure. I won't tap my pencil next time." Commit to the solution.

Let's take another example, using the person drumming their fingers on the desk. I find that extremely annoying.

Here is how the conversation might go:

Rhonda:	I noticed that during the day, without your being aware of it, you drum your fingers on the desk.
You:	Okay. It's just a habit, I've done it for years.
Rhonda:	I know that you don't hear it, but I find it really distracting, and it breaks my concentration, so I'm not as efficient.
You:	Well, I do it without even thinking about it. I'm not even sure why I do it.
Rhonda:	Yes, but it affects me. Can I ask you to not do that? Can I ask you to put something soft under your fingers? Can I . . . ?

I'm offering some solutions.

I'll go back to my old family situation and how I handled that. "I noticed that none of you supported my dad and his wife on their wedding anniversary." I didn't get into why or any of the details (even though I really wanted to). "The reality is my dad now feels completely unsupported by his family. Can I ask you to call him and wish him Happy Anniversary?"

So DESC is a four-step process.

Describe — Here's the situation

Explain — Here's why it's a problem
Solution — Here's what I think a solution might be
Commitment - Can you do that? Yes or no. That's our commitment

Maybe you need to work together to find a solution. Perhaps this is where you collaborate to get to the solution.

When you strategize what it is that you need, all of the other steps are getting you to that point where you know what you need to say, what approach is the right approach, what are you doing that's hurting and what are you doing that's helping.

When you have the conversation, it ends up being a three-minute conversation. It's probably over quickly. You're going to politely say, "How should we fix that?" Literally, within three to five minutes, it's over and you go away, and hopefully everybody's OK with it.

It hasn't been threatening, it hasn't been adversarial. It's been a conversation about, "Let's work together to fix this, and can we do this or not?" That's really, in a perfect world, how a confrontation should be.

Chapter Ten: What is Success?

Strategy. Those who are successful in confrontation know what they want to say. They control their environment as much as they can, but they don't take away the control of the other person.

They control their emotions so that they're not getting carried away. They stick to their mental script of what they want to say. They don't say too much. They don't cause defensiveness in the other person.

It's a very bland, vanilla approach. "Here's the situation. Let's fix the situation," as opposed to, "Here's what you're doing wrong." Although this sounds like a contradiction, they are actually very non-confrontational in a confrontation. It's very strategic, and it's fair and respectful to all parties involved.

When confrontations go wrong, it's usually because the one who starts is too emotional.

They make it all about being right or wrong, and they cause defensiveness in the other person.

Whenever you're having a confrontation, there has to be gray. It's not black or white. There has to be gray, and the willingness to accept that gray and find a solution that works for everybody is the mark of a successful confrontation.

About the Author

Rhonda Scharf is a Certified Speaking Professional who is more than happy to come to your workplace and offer these real-life skills in person. She makes a potentially threatening topic fun, entertaining and easy to deal with. Interaction is a key component of all of her training programs, webinars and keynotes. When you hire Rhonda, your workplace will be a better place!

Since 1993, organizations worldwide have been singing the praises of her programs, such as Dealing with Difficult People, Confrontation Skills and Beat the Bully!

Based in Ottawa, Ontario and Fort Myers, Florida, Rhonda likes to follow the sun when she has time to relax. Regardless of where you are (or where she is), she will gladly come to you.

She is mom and stepmom to three young adults, still part of a blended family, from a blended family, with a very large extended family. Rhonda's real-life stories will entertain you while at the same time teaching you lifelong skills. Dysfunction is no stranger to Rhonda, and she shares how to deal with all the challenges that come from those strange and sometimes unhealthy relationships.

In her spare time, Rhonda and her husband like to travel, golf, run and watch sunsets.

You can contact her at:

Rhonda@on-the-right-track.com

1-877-213-8608

Rhonda has also written **Dealing with Difficult People**, a book you might find complimentary to this one. Order it today at

www.on-the-right-track.com